WILDLIFE VIEWING AREAS

Pennsylvania Ecoregions

- Eastern Great Lakes Lowlands
- North Central Appalachians
- Western Allegheny Plateau
- Ridge and Valley
- Blue Ridge
- Middle Atlantic Coastal Plain
- Erie Drift Plain
- Northern Appalachian Plateau
- Central Appalachians
- Northeastern Highlands
- Northern Piedmont

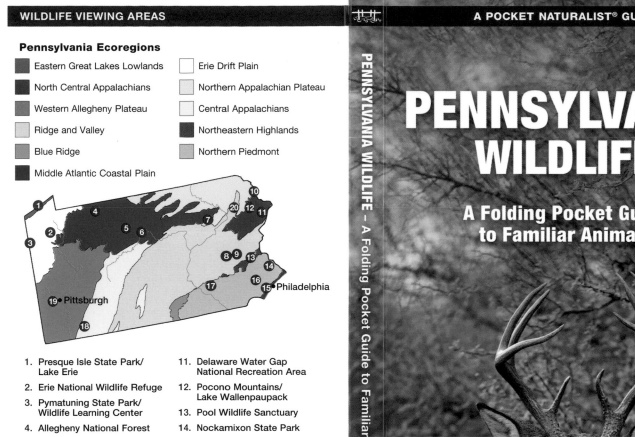

1. Presque Isle State Park/ Lake Erie
2. Erie National Wildlife Refuge
3. Pymatuning State Park/ Wildlife Learning Center
4. Allegheny National Forest
5. Sinnemahoning State Park/Elk State Forest
6. Hyner View State Park/ Sproul State Forest
7. Ricketts Glen State Park/ Glens Natural Area
8. Hawk Mountain Sanctuary
9. Trexler Nature Preserve
10. Upper Delaware National Scenic & Recreational River
11. Delaware Water Gap National Recreation Area
12. Pocono Mountains/ Lake Wallenpaupack
13. Pool Wildlife Sanctuary
14. Nockamixon State Park
15. Philadelphia Zoo
16. John James Audubon Center at Mill Grove
17. Middle Creek Wildlife Management Area
18. Ohiopyle State Park
19. Carnegie Museum of Natural History
20. Everhart Museum of Natural History, Science & Art

Most illustrations show the adult male in breeding coloration. Colors and markings may be duller or absent during different seasons. The measurements denote the length of animals from nose/bill to tail tip. Butterfly measurements denote wingspan. Illustrations are not to scale.

Made in the USA

Waterford Press publishes reference guides to nature observation, outdoor recreation and survival skills. Product information is featured on the website:
www.waterfordpress.com

Text & illustrations © 2009, 2024 Waterford Press Inc. All rights reserved. Photos © Shutterstock. Ecoregion map © The National Atlas of the United States.

To order or for information on custom published products please call 800-434-2555 or email orderdesk@waterfordpress.com. For permissions or to share comments email editor@waterfordpress.com.

ISBN 978-1-58355-483-8 $8.95 U.S.
50895
9 781583 554838
UPC 8 84682 01678 4
10 9 8 7 6 5 4 3 2 1
2400726

PENNSYLVANIA WILDLIFE – A Folding Pocket Guide to Familiar Animals

WATERFORD PRESS

A POCKET NATURALIST® GUIDE

PENNSYLVANIA WILDLIFE

A Folding Pocket Guide to Familiar Animals

T0124007

WATERFORD PRESS

BUTTERFLIES

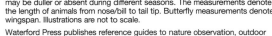

Common Sulphur
Colias philodice
To 2 in. (5 cm)

Black Swallowtail
Papilio polyxenes
To 3.5 in. (9 cm)

Eastern Tiger Swallowtail
Papilio glaucus
To 6 in. (15 cm)

Summer Azure
Celastrina neglecta
To 1 in. (3 cm)

Eastern Tailed Blue
Cupido comyntas
To 1 in. (3 cm)

American Copper
Lycaena phlaeas
To 1.25 in. (3.2 cm)

Underwings
Banded Hairstreak
Satyrium calanus
To 1.25 in. (3.2 cm)

Monarch
Danaus plexippus
To 4 in. (10 cm)

Underwings
Silver-spotted Skipper
Epargyreus clarus
To 2.5 in. (6 cm)

White Admiral
Limenitis arthemis arthemis
To 3 in. (8 cm)

Large Wood Nymph
Cercyonis pegala
To 3 in. (8 cm)

Little Wood Satyr
Megisto cymela
To 2 in. (5 cm)

Pearly Crescentspot
Phyciodes tharos
To 1.5 in. (4 cm)

Great Spangled Fritillary
Speyeria cybele
To 3 in. (8 cm)

Question Mark
Polygonia interrogationis
To 2.5 in. (6 cm)

Mourning Cloak
Nymphalis antiopa
To 3.5 in. (9 cm)

Red Admiral
Vanessa atalanta
To 2.5 in. (6 cm)

INVERTEBRATES

Green Stink Bug
Acrosternum hilare
To .8 in. (2 cm)

Pennsylvania Firefly
Photuris pennsylvanicus
To .8 in. (2 cm)
Pennsylvania's state insect.

Aphid
Family Aphididae
To .5 in. (1.3 cm)
Pear-shaped, soft bodied insect feeds on the sap of plants. Color varies from red and green to black.

Green Lacewings
Family Chrysopidae
To .75 in. (2 cm)
Clear wings have green veins.

Black Carpenter Ant
Camponotus pennsylvanicus
To .5 in. (1.2 cm)

Pennsylvania Leatherwing
Chauliognathus pensylvanicus
To .5 in. (1.2 cm)

House Mosquito
Culex tarsalis
To .25 in (.63 cm)

Honey Bee
Apis mellifera
To .75 in. (2 cm)
Slender bee has pollen baskets on its rear legs.

American House Spider
Parasteatoda tepidariorum
To .25 in. (.6 cm)
Has bulbous, yellow-brown abdomen. Common indoors.

Black-and-yellow Garden Spider
Argiope aurantia
To 1.25 in. (3.2 cm)

German Cockroach
Blattella germanica
To .5 in. (1.3 cm)
Note 2 dark stripes on upper part of thorax. Can climb slick surfaces like glass.

Differential Grasshopper
Melanoplus femur-rubrum
To 1.75 in. (4.5 cm)

Ladybug Beetle
Family Coccinellidae
To .5 in. (1.3 cm)
Red wing covers are black-spotted.

Bumble Bee
Bombus spp.
To 1 in. (3 cm)
Stout, furry bee is large and noisy.

Praying Mantis
Family Mantidae To 2.5 in. (6 cm)
Front legs are held as if praying.

Field Cricket
Gryllus pennsylvanicus To 1 in. (3 cm)
Shrill call is a series of 3 chirps.

FRESHWATER FISHES

Brook Trout
Salvelinus fontinalis To 28 in. (70 cm)
Reddish side spots have blue halos.
Pennsylvania's state fish.

Rainbow Trout
Oncorhynchus mykiss To 44 in. (1.1 m)
Has pink to red side stripe.

Muskellunge
Esox masquinongy To 6 ft. (1.8 m)
Prized sport fish is an aggressive predator.

Redbreast Sunfish
Lepomis auritus To 11 in. (28 cm)
Has narrow, black-tipped ear flap.

Northern Pike
Esox lucius To 53 in. (1.4 m)
Note large head and posterior dorsal fin.

Pumpkinseed
Lepomis gibbosus To 16 in. (40 cm)
Green-orange fish has red-black spot on ear flap.

Smallmouth Bass
Micropterus dolomieu To 27 in. (68 cm)
Jaw joint is beneath the eye.

Black Crappie
Pomoxis nigromaculatus
To 16 in. (40 cm)
Has a humped back and 7-8 dorsal spines.

Largemouth Bass
Micropterus salmoides To 40 in. (1 m)
Jaw joint extends beyond the eye.

Yellow Perch
Perca flavescens To 16 in. (40 cm)
Note 6-9 dark "saddles" down its side.

Bluegill
Lepomis macrochirus To 16 in. (40 cm)

Channel Catfish
Ictalurus punctatus To 4 ft. (1.2 m)
Note prominent "whiskers."

Rock Bass
Ambloplites rupestris To 17 in. (43 cm)
Note red eyes and side blotches.

Walleye
Sander vitreus To 40 in. (1 m)
Note white spot on lower lobe of tail.

REPTILES & AMPHIBIANS

Snapping Turtle
Chelydra serpentina To 18 in. (45 cm)
Note large head, knobby shell and long tail.

Wood Turtle
Glyptemys insculpta To 9 in. (23 cm)
Note sculpted shell and red-orange legs.

Spotted Salamander
Ambystoma maculatum
To 10 in. (25 cm)

Eastern Box Turtle
Terrapene carolina
To 9 in. (23 cm)
Note high-domed shell.

Slimy Salamander
Plethodon glutinosus To 8 in. (20 cm)
Shiny, black skin is covered with light spots.

Five-lined Skink
Plestiodon fasciatus To 8 in. (20 cm)
Has 5 light dorsal stripes.

Milk Snake
Lampropeltis triangulum triangulum
To 7 ft. (2.1 m)

Northern Ringneck Snake
Diadophis punctatus edwardsi
To 30 in. (75 cm)

Common Garter Snake
Thamnophis sirtalis sirtalis
To 4 ft. (1.2 m)
Brownish snake has yellowish back stripes.

Black Rat Snake
Elaphe obsoleta obsoleta To 8 ft. (2.4 m)

Northern Water Snake
Nerodia sipedon To 4.5 ft. (1.4 m)
Note dark blotches on back.

Smooth Green Snake
Opheodrys vernalis To 26 in. (65 cm)

Spring Peeper
Pseudacris crucifer
To 1.5 in. (4 cm)
Note dark X on back. Musical call is a series of short peeps.

Green Frog
Lithobates clamitans
To 4 in. (10 cm)
Single-note call is a banjo-like twang.

Bullfrog
Lithobates catesbeianus
To 8 in. (20 cm)
Call is a deep-pitched – *jug-o-rum*.

American Toad
Anaxyrus americanus
To 4.5 in. (11 cm)
Call is a high musical trill lasting up to 30 seconds.

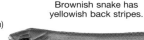

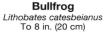

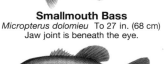

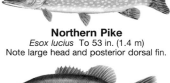

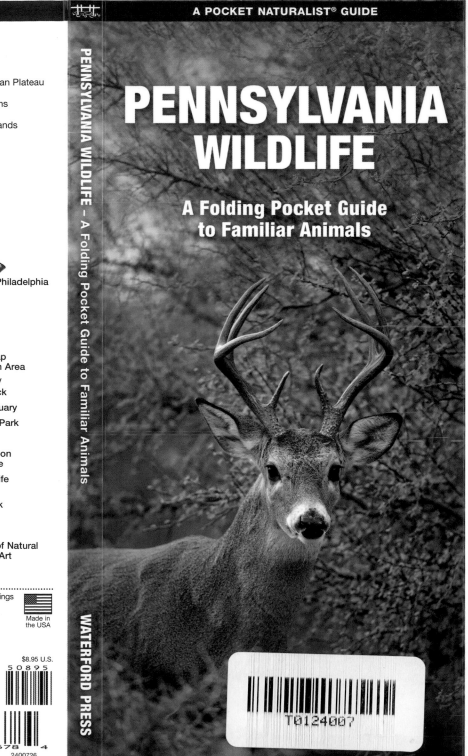

Blue-winged Teal
Spatula discors To 16 in. (40 cm)
Male's white facial crescent is distinctive.

Wood Duck
Aix sponsa To 20 in. (50 cm)

Canada Goose
Branta canadensis
To 43 in. (1.1 m)

Hooded Merganser
Lophodytes cucullatus
To 20 in. (50 cm)
Note white head crest and thin bill.

Pied-billed Grebe
Podilymbus podiceps
To 13 in. (33 cm)

Great Blue Heron
Ardea herodias
To 4.5 ft. (1.4 m)

Killdeer
Charadrius vociferus
To 12 in. (30 cm)
Note two breast bands.

Spotted Sandpiper
Actitis macularius
To 8 in. (20 cm)

Sharp-shinned Hawk
Accipiter striatus
To 14 in. (35 cm)
Note long, square-edged tail and striped breast.

Red-tailed Hawk
Buteo jamaicensis
To 25 in. (63 cm)

Northern Harrier
Circus hudsonius
To 22 in. (55 cm)
Note white rump.

Turkey Vulture
Cathartes aura
To 32 in. (80 cm)

Cooper's Hawk
Accipiter cooperii
To 20 in. (50 cm)
Note long, rounded tail.

Bald Eagle
Haliaeetus leucocephalus
To 40 in. (1 m)

American Kestrel
Falco sparverius
To 12 in. (30 cm)
Note small size and blue wings.

Great Horned Owl
Bubo virginianus
To 25 in. (63 cm)
Call is a resonant –
hoo-HOO-hoooo.

Barred Owl
Strix varia
To 2 ft. (60 cm)
Call is a rhythmic –
who-cooks-for-you.

Ring-necked Pheasant
Phasianus colchicus
To 3 ft. (90 cm)

Rock Pigeon
Columba livia
To 13 in. (33 cm)

Ruffed Grouse
Bonasa umbellus
To 14 in. (35 cm)
Note black tail band.
Pennsylvania's state game bird.

Wild Turkey
Meleagris gallopavo
To 4 ft. (1.2 m)

Mourning Dove
Zenaida macroura
To 13 in. (33 cm)

Downy Woodpecker
Dryobates pubescens
To 6 in. (15 cm)
The similar hairy woodpecker is larger and has a longer bill.

Pileated Woodpecker
Dryocopus pileatus
To 17 in. (43 cm)
Note large size.

Northern Flicker
Colaptes auratus
To 13 in. (33 cm)
Wing and tail linings are yellow.

Ruby-throated Hummingbird
Archilochus colubris
To 3.5 in. (9 cm)

Red-bellied Woodpecker
Melanerpes carolinus

Belted Kingfisher
Megaceryle alcyon
To 14 in. (35 cm)

Carolina Wren
Thryothorus ludovicianus
To 6 in. (15 cm)
Note white eyebrow stripe and wing bars.

American Crow
Corvus brachyrhynchos
To 22 in. (55 cm)

Tufted Titmouse
Baeolophus bicolor
To 6 in. (15 cm)

Blue Jay
Cyanocitta cristata
To 14 in. (35 cm)

White-breasted Nuthatch
Sitta carolinensis
To 6 in. (15 cm)

Eastern Bluebird
Sialia sialis
To 7 in. (18 cm)

American Robin
Turdus migratorius
To 11 in. (28 cm)

Northern Cardinal
Cardinalis cardinalis
To 9 in. (23 cm)

European Starling
Sturnus vulgaris
To 8 in. (20 cm)

Red-winged Blackbird
Agelaius phoeniceus
To 9 in. (23 cm)

Cedar Waxwing
Bombycilla cedrorum
To 7 in. (18 cm)
Red wing marks look like waxy droplets.

Northern Mockingbird
Mimus polyglottos
To 11 in. (28 cm)

Song Sparrow
Melospiza melodia
To 7 in. (18 cm)
Note central breast spot.

Brown Creeper
Certhia americana
To 5 in. (13 cm)
Forages for insects on tree trunks.

American Goldfinch
Spinus tristis
To 5 in. (13 cm)

House Finch
Haemorhous mexicanus
To 6 in. (15 cm)

House Sparrow
Passer domesticus
To 6 in. (15 cm)

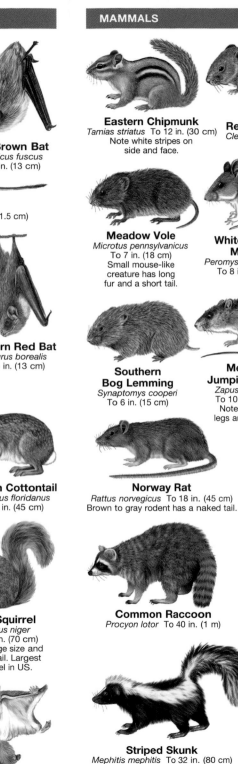

Virginia Opossum
Didelphis virginiana
To 40 in. (1 m)
Note long tail and naked tail.

Northern Short-tailed Shrew
Blarina brevicauda
To 5 in. (13 cm)
Venomous.

Big Brown Bat
Eptesicus fuscus
To 5 in. (13 cm)

Masked Shrew
Sorex cinereus To 4.5 in. (11.5 cm)
Note pointed nose.

Star-nosed Mole
Condylura cristata
To 8 in. (20 cm)
Nose has 22 fleshy, finger-like projections.

Little Brown Bat
Myotis lucifugus
To 3.5 in. (9 cm)

Hoary Bat
Lasiurus cinereus
To 6 in. (15 cm)
Brown fur is white-tipped.

Eastern Red Bat
Lasiurus borealis
To 5 in. (13 cm)

Summer   Winter

Snowshoe Hare
Lepus americanus To 20 in. (50 cm)
Found in the Appalachian uplands. Coat is white in winter.

Eastern Cottontail
Sylvilagus floridanus
To 18 in. (45 cm)

Red Squirrel
Tamiasciurus hudsonicus
To 14 in. (35 cm)
Squirrel is rusty red above and whitish below.

Eastern Gray Squirrel
Sciurus carolinensis
To 20 in. (50 cm)

Fox Squirrel
Sciurus niger
To 28 in. (70 cm)
Note large size and bushy tail. Largest squirrel in US.

Southern Flying Squirrel
Glaucomys volans
To 10 in. (25 cm)

Eastern Chipmunk
Tamias striatus To 12 in. (30 cm)
Note white stripes on side and face.

Southern Red-backed Vole
Clethrionomys gapperi
To 6 in. (15 cm)

Groundhog
Marmota monax
To 32 in. (80 cm)
Also called woodchuck. Resident Punxsutawney Phil "predicts" the length of winter on Groundhog Day, Feb. 2.

Meadow Vole
Microtus pennsylvanicus
To 7 in. (18 cm)
Small mouse-like creature has long fur and a short tail.

White-footed Mouse
Peromyscus leucopus
To 8 in. (20 cm)

House Mouse
Mus musculus
To 8 in. (20 cm)
Introduced pest has a naked tail.

Southern Bog Lemming
Synaptomys cooperi
To 6 in. (15 cm)

Meadow Jumping Mouse
Zapus hudsonius
To 10 in. (25 cm)
Note long hind legs and long tail.

Deer Mouse
Peromyscus maniculatus
To 8 in. (20 cm)
Distinguished by white undersides and hairy tail.

Norway Rat
Rattus norvegicus To 18 in. (45 cm)
Brown to gray rodent has a naked tail.

Common Muskrat
Ondatra zibethicus To 2 ft. (60 cm)
Aquatic rodent has a naked tail that is flattened on its sides.

Common Raccoon
Procyon lotor To 40 in. (1 m)

Striped Skunk
Mephitis mephitis To 32 in. (80 cm)

Common Porcupine
Erethizon dorsatum To 3 ft. (90 cm)

Northern River Otter
Lontra canadensis
To 52 in. (1.3 m)

American Beaver
Castor canadensis
To 4 ft. (1.2 m)

Long-tailed Weasel
Mustela frenata To 21 in. (53 cm)
Note brown feet and yellowish neck.

Short-tailed Weasel
Mustela erminea To 14 in. (35 cm)
Note white feet. Coat may turn white in winter. Also known as ermine.

Common Gray Fox
Urocyon cinereoargenteus
To 3.5 ft. (1.1 m)
Note black-tipped tail.

Mink
Neovison vison
To 28 in. (70 cm)
Chin is white.

Red Fox
Vulpes vulpes To 40 in. (1 m)
Note white-tipped tail.

Coyote
Canis latrans To 52 in. (1.3 m)
Note bushy, black-tipped tail.

Black Bear
Ursus americanus
To 6 ft. (1.8 m)

Bobcat
Lynx rufus To 4 ft. (1.2 m)

White-tailed Deer
Odocoileus virginianus
To 7 ft. (2.1 m)
Pennsylvania's state animal.

Elk
Cervus canadensis
To 10 ft. (3 m)
Widely reintroduced to the state.